Head, Heart & Hands

With kind regards, ॐ and prem

Head, Heart & Hand

Head, Heart & Hands

Swami Niranjanananda Saraswati

*Discourses from the Yogadrishti (Yogavision) series
of satsangs at Ganga Darshan Vishwa Yogapeeth,
Munger, from 9th to 12th October 2010*

Yoga Publications Trust, Munger, Bihar, India

Published by Yoga Publications Trust
    First edition 2011

ISBN: 978-81-86336-98-4

Ganga Darshan,

Butala Emporium, New York
Tel : (718) 899-5590
Online @ www.indousplaza.com
Email : service@indousplaza.com

Printed at Aegean Offset Printers, Greater Noida

Dedication

To our guru Sri Swami Satyananda Saraswati
who continues to inspire and guide us
on our spiritual journey.

Contents

Creation and Transcendence

9 October 2010

Every human being comes into this world endowed with three faculties: head, heart and hands. Most people do not utilize these faculties properly or understand their potential. In order to cultivate these three powers, one has to first understand what they mean. One has to understand the inherent qualities, possibilities and potentials of these three faculties, and the effort that one can make to awaken them.

Creation according to tantra and Samkhya

Tantra speaks of two realities: consciousness and energy. It states that the whole creation is nothing but an interplay, exchange and interaction between consciousness and energy – different manifestations and forms of consciousness and energy. Energy is known as Shakti and consciousness as Shiva. It is possible that once upon a time Shiva and Shakti were real people who propagated the subject of tantra, but the story is so ancient that it is difficult to ascertain the facts. The concept of Shiva and Shakti in tantra pertains to consciousness and energy. Therefore, when the words Shiva and Shakti are used in tantra, do not confuse them with the images and forms of Shiva and Shakti.

In ancient times, the sages and seers understood that what every individual expresses in life is nothing but an expression of consciousness and energy, which are inherent in the body, nature and personality. At the same time, they are

1

interconnected with the cosmic consciousness and energy. There is a link and association between the consciousness inherent in the individual and the consciousness pervading the cosmos, between the energy in the individual and the energy that pervades the cosmos. Since all beings come from the same source, it can be said that the cosmic consciousness is contained within the human nature and personality in a minuscule part.

Shakti is the active or dynamic principle and Shiva is the passive principle. Consciousness is the passive principle and energy is the active principle. When creation takes place, there is a permutation and combination of consciousness and energy at the cosmic level. What comes forth through this process is the greater mind. This concept takes one into the Samkhya system.

The greater mind, developed from the permutation and combination of consciousness and energy, is known as *mahat*. Mahat is composed of four different states of experience: *ahamkara* or ego, *buddhi* or intelligence, *chitta* or the inner mind where memories are contained, and *manas* or the reflective rational mind. The four together, working in unison and harmony, are identified as the greater mind. The distinction between them is felt only when any one state becomes predominant and is felt as an independent experience. According to tantra, at the cosmic level, consciousness and energy, Shiva and Shakti, live in harmony with each other. They exist as one. When they separate, when energy separates from consciousness or consciousness separates from energy, creation takes place.

When energy separates from consciousness, it has to function on its own and there is nothing to guide the function or role of energy. Our guru, Sri Swami Satyananda, gives an example: a blind person and a lame person are friends. They want to go to a fair. How do they go? The blind man cannot see but has full use of the legs; the lame man cannot walk but has full use of the eyes. Therefore, they help each other out. The lame one sits on the shoulders of the blind

one and guides the way. He says, "Go forward, watch out for that hole, for that bump, turn right, turn left, there is a slope here, there is an incline there." The blind one follows the instructions of the lame one and continues to walk. Shiva and Shakti, consciousness and energy, exist in a parallel situation. Tantra says that consciousness is lame; it cannot walk but can see. Energy is blind; it cannot see, perceive, rationalize or understand but can move.

When consciousness and energy are together, they function in harmony and unison with each other and there is absolute bliss and peace. When they separate, when the lame one comes down from the shoulders of the blind one and has to function on his own, the effect is different. The quality and expression of Shakti changes. Consciousness becomes aloof, introverted and withdrawn, while Shakti becomes the active principle. When Shakti becomes the active principle, creation takes place. The first evolute to manifest in the process of creation is mahat, which is constituted of four aspects: manas, buddhi, chitta and ahamkara.

In the course of creation, *tattwas* or elements also manifest. They constitute the body, which is a result of the combination and permutation of the five tattwas. If you observe individual natures, the presence of the tattwas will be evident. Some people are full of air, some are fire, some are water, some are space and some are earthy. When a tattwa is predominant, its character is reflected in the behaviour of the individual. What is pertinent is that these elements create the body. They create the senses and interact with the created world or dimension. It is due to the tattwas that human beings are functioning in the created dimension and not the invisible dimension. The created dimension can be understood by the senses and the mind. You can touch a metallic object and feel its coolness and hardness. The senses are interacting with the created world, the environment, the world of sense objects. The mind is interacting with the environment, desires, associations, people, needs; it is interacting with attributes that are necessary for survival. Without these, you cannot awaken spiritual understanding or awareness.

Spiritual awareness
Spiritual awareness is different from religious awareness. Spirituality has nothing to do with religion and religion has nothing to do with spirituality; they are two different paths altogether. People believe that by following a religion one can become spiritual, but that is not right. Spiritual awareness or spiritual realization is a personal experience. It is a personal effort to improve the quality of life. Therefore, a distinction must be made between spirituality and religiosity.

4

From the tantric and yogic perspective, to be spiritual means to become aware of the luminous qualities inherent in you. People believe that they can become spiritual if they practise meditation. Wrong. People believe they can become spiritual if they follow a religion. Wrong. People believe they can become spiritual if they practise a mantra or think of God and worship God. Wrong. All this is not spirituality. You cannot acquire spirituality through meditation, contemplation, worship or any other such effort. Spirituality has to be discovered within yourself, and that is the process of yoga and tantra. The spiritual nature is beyond the world of senses and sense objects. The spiritual experience transcends the body and mind experience.

The understanding of spiritual life or the spiritual quality is acquired through a process of observation and modification of the normal behaviour patterns of life. Remember that one does not become spiritual by contemplation, meditation, ritual or worship, but by following one's dharma. That is one point that everyone misses. Nobody follows their dharma, but everybody tries to meditate.

People come to me and ask, "How can I become spiritual?" I tell them, "First stop criticizing others. First stop being destructive in your own mind, stop being aggressive in your own nature." They say, "Should I meditate?" I say, "No, that is not necessary. You don't need meditation to discover your spiritual nature." They look at me disbelievingly, as they have always heard, "Meditate and you will experience divinity, luminosity." Everyone has been told that the aim of life is to attain self-realization or God-realization. It is this expectation that motivates people to discover the God inside. The God inside cannot be discovered, at least not by people mired in material life in this age. People don't have that character, that sankalpa shakti, that zeal, that fixity of mind. Therefore, they can meditate, but never see God or realize the Self. This indicates that there is a big flaw in their understanding of how to integrate and incorporate the practices to attain the higher experience.

What I am saying applies to everyone, whether they are sannyasins or sadhakas. Sannyasa does not make anyone spiritual; yoga does not make anyone spiritual. It is understanding one's own nature, modifying one's behaviour patterns, understanding one's dharma and adhering to the precepts of dharma that makes one spiritual.

Tantra: path of qualitative change in life

Tantra has always maintained that the path of spirituality is the path of transformation of the personality. Tantra is asking you to change the quality of life, by following a system and a path, by adhering to a process. The tantric systems describe the methods of overcoming the difficulties and sufferings of life. In tantra, Parvati asks Shiva, the teacher, "Pray tell me, not how to become enlightened, but how to overcome the pain and suffering of life." Shiva proceeds to tell her the process of alleviating suffering and pain in life. After the removal of suffering, the new you experiences a new mind, and that new mind is the higher or cosmic mind.

All this is attainable while living in this body and world. It is possible to acquire a new mind, and that is what you have to strive for. Tantra has always been clear that you have to face your limitations in life. Your senses, knowledge and intelligence are limited; your ego, smriti and buddhi are conditioned. You live in this conditioned nature and experience joy and happiness, pain and suffering, but if there is a desire to discover something else within, then it is necessary to go through the process of sadhana.

Discovering sat-chit-ananda

The tradition says that you have to discover three experiences within yourself. First, *sat*, truth or reality. You have to know what is real, you have to discover the truth in everything. Second, *chit*, the experience that consciousness is able to expand and outgrow its self-imposed limitations and boundaries. Third, *ananda*, the experience that there is no suffering and pain in life, only bliss. Thus, sat, chit and ananda are the three experiences that have to be discovered in life. This completes the journey of life, for in that state of realization of sat-chit-ananda, all dual behaviours and natures drop away. All the understandings and misunderstandings which create the concept of right and wrong drop away, and one becomes established in truth, in bliss and in the expanded awareness. That state of realization is identified by tantra as the ultimate aspiration of a human being. That is what one needs to acquire, achieve and experience.

The entire subject of tantra is the discovery of sat, chit and ananda. What is the underlying truth? How can one cultivate the expanded awareness and be permanently immersed in the blissful state? Yoga, which has emerged from tantra, follows this idea. When Sage Patanjali speaks of samadhi, he describes it not as one static condition or state of mind, but as progressive conditions and stages of mind. In these progressive stages, the gross mind is gradually tran-

scended and transformed and one becomes more and more stable in the higher mind. When one becomes stable in the higher mind, sat, chit and ananda are experienced. This is the theory of tantra: consciousness and energy in the course of time become life as it is experienced. This life is limited and confined by the senses and conditions of the mind. In order to experience the expansiveness of consciousness, to know the truth, the reality behind life, creation, destruction and dissolution, one has to follow the path of sat, chit and ananda. The process which gives an expression to the awareness of sat, chit and ananda in life is yoga.

Nature of samsara

Samkhya defines the progression of evolution from the very beginning of creation. It describes the formation of manifest elements and forces from subtle elements and forces: ahamkara, ego; buddhi, intelligence; chitta, memory field; manas, reflective ability; *indriyas*, senses; *tattwas*, elements; *tanmatras*, essence of the elements; *gunas*, qualities. They are all consequent manifestations in creation through which the individual identifies with the world in which he is living.

If you did not possess the senses, you would not be able to associate with your environment or the world. If you did not possess the greater mind, you would not be able to appreciate the expressions of manas, buddhi, chitta and ahamkara. Thus, everything that you come equipped with in this life is only geared for material life. If God wanted you to be enlightened from day one, He would not have given you a tamasic nature, He would not have given you *vasanas*, desires and ambitions, He would not have given you envy, jealousy and greed. Rather, He would have given you those attributes by which you could easily evolve into a higher state of being.

The nature of the world is such that it impedes the path of evolution. No matter how hard you try in spiritual life, you will always find some block or barrier linked with the external world. Whether it is your family, society or a professional problem, something will divert your mind out into the world again. Association with the world creates attachment, and the nature of the senses and the mind is to become attached. The senses always look for something pleasing and reject that which is unpleasant. The mind always looks for something pleasing and entertaining to make itself happy and is bored without entertainment. In this way, all the equipment that you possess is geared to interacting with the world.

Exit points from samsara

Despite the human predisposition to attach to samsara, an escape route has been left open so that those who do not want to live in the world can identify with something different. It is an outlet to get out of the world, just as every house has an exit door. If you don't like living in the house, just get out of the door. In the same manner, there is an outlet, an exit point from this world. That exit point is identified in three ways: first, when you experience an intense desire to discover happiness within; second, when you find a guru; third, when the guru slaps you. When you make a mistake, the guru has to correct you and if you have trust, belief and faith in the guru, you will abide by the instructions. That opens the door of exit wider.

1. **Intensity of desire for transcendence**: To find an exit point from samsara, first the desire must be there. There is a story about Ramakrishna Paramahamsa. One day, a seeker came to him and said, "I want to have darshan of the Mother. You are able to commune with Mother. Why don't you ask Her to give me darshan?" Ramakrishna did not answer. The person continued to pester him, but Ramakrishna remained silent. Finally, it was evening and Ramakrishna rose to his feet and went for a bath in the river. The man also followed him and said, "You haven't given me an answer." Ramakrishna said, "All right, first come and take a bath, then I will give you the answer." The seeker thought, "Wonderful! I am going to receive my answer after the bath." He jumped into the water. As soon as he was in the water, Ramakrishna grabbed him by the neck and forced his head under water. Of course the

man began to choke. He began to gasp and sputter, flailing his arms and legs in desperation, but Ramakrishna just sat on his shoulders. Eventually the man became so agitated that in one mighty push he threw Ramakrishna off, broke free and took a deep breath. At that point Ramakrishna said to him, "When your desire to have darshan is as intense as this, only then will you have darshan, not otherwise." What he said to the seeker has been true for all times.

There is a difference between curiosity and intensity of feeling. Most people experiment with spiritual life out of curiosity, "Let us see what this new thing is." They don't come with intensity of feeling. If curiosity is the base, it is very flimsy. After fifteen days you become bored and say, "This ashram is not nice, I'll go to another ashram and practise lots of hatha yoga." You become bored with this ashram after twenty days, saying, "Ah, too much! My body is aching all over. Now I need to practise some Ayurveda." So you go to Kerala for a nice massage. After the limbs are limbered up a bit, you say, "Let me try vinyasa while I am in this city." You go to vinyasa yoga and after some time you say, "The teacher is no good, I will go home."

Every association in your life is out of curiosity. People even take sannyasa out of curiosity, not because they feel committed to it. If the intensity was there, none of the head trips that aspiring sannyasins go through would be there. If there was intensity in what you believe in, have faith in and are aspiring for, then all the head trips you undergo would be eliminated. They are a result of curiosity, why this and why that, why can't I and why can't you, the syndrome of 'you have and I don't have'. It's a very petty-minded syndrome of a mind which is always comparing, desiring and is curious. Intensity of desire is the first requirement.

2. **Finding a guru**: The second exit point is discovered by finding a guru. How do you find a guru? Do you search in the Yellow Pages and call the one with the biggest advertisement? Is he the big guru and the one with a one-line advertisement a small guru? And the one with no advertisement is no guru!

Guru is a person with whom you feel a spiritual connection. Somebody once asked me, "Can you be my guru? I am still searching for a guru." I asked him, "What are you searching for in the guru? Do you want your guru to be a six-footer or a four-footer? Do you want your guru to be fat or slim? What are you searching for?" The reply was, "Compatibility." I said, "What kind of compatibility? Intellectual? You will never become intellectually compatible with the guru because his understanding is different from yours. Emotional? Not possible, because the emotions of the guru are different from yours." He said, "Somebody who can guide me." I said, "Before you try to find somebody who can guide you, discover whether you are willing to follow the instructions."

This is the reality. Guru is a guide, somebody who can inspire you and tell you what to do for the development of your spiritual life, but there has to be a proper understanding and awareness of your spiritual need. Guru is a spiritual guide, not a social guide. He is not a marriage consultant. He is not a psychologist who can solve your psychological problems. He is not a financial analyst who can solve your financial problems. He is not a marriage counsellor who can tell you who to marry and who not to.

The relationship with the guru is sacred. It is a personal matter, not a subject of gossip. When you gossip away what your guru has told you, it is because your relationship is not clear, and therefore you can never progress. If the sanctity of the relationship is there, then a close connection develops, which is not intellectual, mental or emotional. It is spiritual. It is this connection that has to develop between guru and disciple, for that is what opens the exit door from the material world into the spiritual dimension.

3. Slap of guru: If you analyze your life, it revolves around a few things only: family, friends, profession and society. These are the major areas of concern in everybody's life. No matter what you do, a link is maintained with these aspects all the time. Even in meditation there is a link with family, friends and society. That link is never broken. They are thick ropes pulling you to the side of the external world, and one small string of spiritual life is trying to pull you to the other side. Which is stronger? The little thread of spiritual life gets broken very easily and the thick ropes of family, friends, society and profession pull you back to ground level.

When this happens, the slap of the guru is needed. The guru has to come in and say, "Identify your aspirations once again." If you are truthful to your aspirations, then you have to somehow cut the ropes that pull you back to the gross plane, but if your material aspirations are more powerful, then forget spiritual life. Live the material life and fulfil your samskaras and karmas.

Spiritual life and material life cannot coexist, just as day and night cannot coexist and oil and water cannot mix. Material and spiritual cannot come together. Water is water, oil is oil; day is day, night is night and the twain shall never meet.

Altering the material mentality

The gross or material mentality has to be altered. Tantra says the material mentality can be altered by cultivating the positive and benevolent qualities in life. The qualities that are usually expressed in the material world in the course of interactions are anger, jealousy, envy, hatred, greed, avarice, lethargy and such like. However, when spiritual awareness begins to dawn, these destructive and limiting behaviours have to dissolve and the positive powers of life have to awaken. The positive powers of life include love, compassion, sympathy and understanding. The greatest positive power in life is understanding, not even love. Love is only an expression, understanding is a power. With understanding comes love; in the absence of understanding there is no love. Understandii.g is the highest quality that one can possess.

When there is understanding and a clear mind, one can achieve anything in life. All the problems in family and society arise because of lack of understanding. Misunderstanding takes place between two people and problems occur. Even newlyweds, only two people living in a house, can have a

misunderstanding. What does this indicate? That there is a part of your nature which is rigid and does not seek to understand, only enforce its own will. When you try to enforce your own will without understanding, conflicts arise. Therefore, tantra says that understanding is the key quality which allows the positive and soft attributes to germinate in life. Spiritual awareness comes not with meditation, but with cultivation of understanding.

Head, heart and hands

All the aspects of your nature have to be managed to cultivate the faculties of head, heart and hands. The yogic journey is about how you deal with your consciousness, manage your energies, cultivate small things to enhance the ability of the mind, open up the heart and bring creativity to the hands.

Probiotic Yoga

10 October 2010

From the tantric perspective, the two realities known as Shiva and Shakti are consciousness and energy. The ancients used the terms Shiva and Shakti because that was the language they had at that time. They also came to the conclusion that when these two powers or realities remain together in harmony, there is no creation, there is only pure existence: of truth, consciousness and bliss. Creation takes place when Shiva and Shakti, consciousness and energy, separate from each other and become independently active. The material creation is an outcome of Shakti being independent of Shiva.

Roles of Shakti and Shiva

The pure primordial Shakti, the original Shakti, has a name: Yogamaya. The word *yogamaya* contains two concepts. It is made up of two words: yoga and maya. *Yoga* means coming together, coming closer, joining and uniting, while *maya* means separation and delusion. Thus, the cosmic energy, Shakti, has two roles to play: one as the yogic power and the other as the maya power. In the interplay of Shakti in life, both possibilities are seen: going in the direction of yoga or in the direction of maya. If you choose to go in the direction of yoga, union, then you are utilizing that energy to return to the source. If you go towards maya for enjoyment, then maya separates you from the source or creates more distance between you and the source. This is the role of the primordial Shakti.

15

Just as Shakti is named Yogamaya, Shiva is named Satchitananda, indicating that it contains three aspects: truth, consciousness and bliss. Where there is truth, there is consciousness and bliss; there is wholeness, completeness and self-contentment. It is the expanding or evolving consciousness which realizes the truth and permanent bliss. Thus Shiva has the name Satchitananda and Shakti has the name Yogamaya. These names indicate the potential and possibility inherent in Shiva and Shakti, and what they can lead one to.

When Shiva and Shakti separate from each other, then distinction takes place. There is no cosmic harmony any more. Independent identities are created – this is Shiva and that is Shakti, this is the role of Shiva and that is the role of Shakti. Creation begins when Shakti separates from Shiva, but Shiva also has a role to play in creation. Shakti in itself is incapable of creation, because energy has no perception, understanding, vision or sight. Shiva has the vision and sight, but is unable to act or perform because it is limbless. It is just a state of being. I gave the example of the blind man and lame man wanting to go to a fair. The lame guides the blind and the blind carries the lame and they reach their destination. In the same manner, Shiva and Shakti assist each other in creation.

The contribution of Shiva in creation is subtle: it manifests as *mahat*, the great mind. Mahat has four compartments: *ahamkara*, ego; *chitta*, psyche, where latent impressions are stored; *buddhi*, intelligence; *manas*, reflective power. This is the role of Shiva. Shakti is responsible for the creation of elements, *panchabhootas*, *pancha tattwas*, *pancha tanmatras*. Anything that is material in nature is created by Shakti. She creates the five elements, and the permutation and combination of the five elements create universes, galaxies and life forms. The human being is a result of this combination of elements; the body is an outcome of the combination of the five elements. Shakti is also responsible for the creation of the material world of the senses and sense objects. The role of Shiva comes to a stop after the emergence of mahat. That is the subtle creation, while the gross creation is due to Shakti.

Attributes of the created human being

The point of discussion now directly relates to you, so try to understand it properly. If creation is made up of the five elements, then the body is also made up of the five elements. If creation was only ethereal, then the body would also be only ethereal. If creation was only fire, then the body would also have the form and shape of fire. If creation was only water, then life forms would also be water based. What this means is that every life form is adjusted by Shakti to survive and live in its own natural environment. Life forms of water cannot survive on land, life forms of land cannot survive in water and will burn in fire, life forms of fire will perish if they are in water. There are many dimensions in the universe and even planets where different kinds of life forms exist, not necessarily in this kind of body, but as elemental spirits, forces and entities.

When the life form is adapted to live in its own environment, the greater mind becomes active and specific attributes come into play.

Self-identity: The first attribute is ahamkara. When ahamkara becomes active, the awareness that 'this is me' comes in, the awareness that 'I exist' is realized. That is self-identity, the first expression of ahamkara. Since 'I exist', all the attributes of 'my' ahamkara are based on the instinct of survival. The awareness that 'I exist' as a person, as a being, is the identity of ahamkara. All the expressions of ahamkara are orientated and geared to self-preservation in the form of instinct. Therefore, the instinct of self-preservation is the strongest.

Self-preservation is preservation of the body, mind, family, friends and society. Nobody wants to see their house fall down, their body sick, their family or society in distress. If there is health, peace and beauty everywhere, then everyone is contented. But when there is illness – personal, social and external – the human psyche becomes disturbed. That is the expression of ahamkara. Instincts over which there is no control, an instinct which you cannot guide and channel is ahamkara; it is an attribute that only satisfies your own self.

The four basic instincts are *ahara* or craving, *nidra* or sleep, *bhaya* or insecurity, *maithuna* or sexuality and sensuality. The basis of craving is satisfaction of one's needs, and the two main cravings are food to nourish the body and happiness to nourish the mind. Of course, you can attach yourself to anything and crave it, but that craving is different from the craving of self-preservation. One cannot survive in the world without food and mental stimulation. Ahara is the first response of the manifest ego: nourish the body, nourish the mind, become comfortable, know that this is you. That is when you are happy, relaxed, healthy and contented.

Psyche: The second attribute of mahat is chitta, the psyche or the deeper mind where impressions of the past are stored. Consciousness is continuously evolving. You remember events of your childhood or events that took place many years ago. At every stage of your life, you accumulate memories which are stored in the hard drive of the brain – sometimes easily accessible and sometimes requiring a search through the old files and folders of the hard disk since you don't use them frequently. When the latent impressions in consciousness are carried forward, they become samskaras and karmas. Memories of the past manifest in the future either as karma or samskara. Thus, instincts are an outcome of ahamkara, whereas karmas, samskaras and *vasanas*, obsessive desires, are an outcome of chitta.

Faculty of recognition of environment: Buddhi is the third attribute of mahat. It connects one with the environment in which one lives. There is recognition of the environment, followed by its acceptance or rejection. It is not the intellect as you know it, but the original universal faculty which identifies life with the environment in which it exists. It identifies the physical senses with sense objects all around. It creates an association between senses and sense objects, between the mind and the world. That is the role of buddhi.

When you touch something, say, a microphone, the personal senses are contacting an external object. It is buddhi which is analyzing the object and saying, "It is hard, cold, stiff, moveable, big, small, soft, smooth, it has grooves." Such understanding of an object takes place through buddhi. The same process is followed in sight. If you looked at someone and buddhi was not there, you would not know that you were looking at a person, you could be looking at a blank wall. Due to the presence of buddhi, you can identify what you are seeing as a person. The senses are guided by buddhi. Taste, smell, touch, vision, hearing are all guided by buddhi. The senses and buddhi come together to create an understanding of the external world.

Rationality: Manas is the fourth aspect of mahat. It has a limited role, as it cannot survive without the inputs of ego, chitta and buddhi. Manas will reflect upon the inputs of these three. Beyond that, it does not have any role. The rationalities only relate to things that are emerging in the field of manas due to ahamkara, buddhi and chitta. When you think of something, what are you thinking about? From where has that thought arrived? It has come either from buddhi, chitta or ahamkara and that is what you are reflecting upon.

If somebody does you harm, it is ahamkara which tells you that this person has harmed you and you need to react. Manas will only think about the harm inflicted by that person and how you can react because of the input from ahamkara. For a person engaged in developing finances, the input will come from buddhi and then manas will think about it. Similarly, chitta may bring up an old memory and plant it in the forefront of your mind and manas will then begin to think about that event. Therefore, manas actualizes the events that take place in ahamkara, buddhi and chitta. This idea is different from the prototype theory of manas.

Lower mind and greater mind

The four faculties of ahamkara, buddhi, chitta and manas constitute the Shiva or consciousness aspect. They become the lower mind in material life when they are associating with the world of sense objects. When they are freed from the world of sense objects, they become the greater mind. It is similar to being in the confines of a room.

When you are in the confines of a room, your perception is only that of the room and not of what exists outdoors. However, when you leave the room and go out into the open, you use the same senses, the same mind, but your perspective, vision, understanding, appreciation, everything changes. The same mind and the senses behave differently when confined and when freed. The confined state is the state of the lower mind and the freed state is the state of the higher mind.

Association with sense objects

There is a point at which the senses and sense objects connect. There is a natural and mutual attraction, which alters the nature of the mind. A desire is created: "I want it." If the object had no influence on your mind, it would not alter your mind. You would say, "I don't need it." But when it alters the nature of the mind, you begin to desire that object. For example, you notice a beautiful flower in a vase and the thought comes: "Can I take it with me?" That simple sentence

20

indicates that the object has somehow influenced your mind. If it was not attractive to you, it would lay there and you would not even look at it. However, since you looked at it, a link, an association, a desire was created. This desire is created due to the association of the senses and sense objects.

Sri Krishna says in the *Bhagavad Gita* (2:62–63): *Sangaat sanjaayate kaamah* – "When connected with sense objects, the mind gives birth to desire." Desire becomes attachment. Desire has two forms. One is the superficial desire, "It would be nice if I could have it." But when desire becomes a craving, more intense and deeper, then attachment is created. Day and night, you think about the object which has become a piece of your mental attachment. When the desire is not attainable, yet you want it, you become aggressive: *Kaamaat krodhobhijaayate*. When you become aggressive, the mind is deluded: *Krodhaad bhavati sammohah*. The desire to possess becomes more dominant and prominent, and you lose touch with clarity of mind and reality. This is the deluded state of mind which is obsessed by one thought, influenced by one desire, event or object: *Sammohaat smriti vibhramah*. When the mind is deluded in such a manner, then rationality and understanding have no role in life and you lose touch with reality, that is the death of intelligence: *Smritibhranshaat buddhinaasho, buddhinaashaat pranashyati*. When does intelligence die? When you lose contact with reality and live in a fantasy or deluded world.

It is the association with sense objects which begins as a desire and becomes attachment, due to which you confuse all your virtues and vices with desires and attachments. Passion and sexuality are seen as love, although they are not. Sensuality is identified as love, although it is not. When you tell a person you love them, so what do you love in that person? You don't know the character of the person, so what do you love in that person? The body. You don't even know the nature of the person, what do you love of that person? You don't love their nature or character. You love the beauty and the body of the person and that becomes your craving. After marriage, when you discover the other side, then divorce takes place. If you had discovered the other side before marriage, maybe you would not have married the person in the first place. People have not arrived at the real nature of love. They have only encountered physical love and passion in their life, and identified that with the ultimate understanding of love.

Love is something that you have never experienced in life. You have experienced passion: physical, mental and emotional. You have experienced infatuation, but you have not experienced love. You have confused infatuation, passion and obsession with love. Love cannot be experienced without acquiring understanding. Understanding has to come first and love comes next.

Your ideas of love are notions generated in the mind in relation to external things or sense objects only. They are caused by association of the mind with sense objects. A husband or a wife is a sense object, nothing more. That is the core of the problem. Existing in this material life and seeing everything around, naturally there is a desire to possess and experience personal satisfaction. This personal satisfaction is often guided by envy, jealousy, need or necessity. If your competitor acquires a better car than you, if you have an old Ambassador and your competitor Mr X acquires a Mercedes, then out of envy you will attach yourself to a better model. The desire for it will become your need. However, that perceived need is guided by your jealousy; it is not your real need.

When people indulge in comparison: "You have that and I don't have it," it is due to jealousy and envy. This envy and jealousy is materialistic because you are only seeing the external attributes. Who knows, maybe internally you are far better than the person you are trying to compete with! However, you don't look at that. You only look at the clothes the other person is wearing and identify with the desire to wear better clothes. You look at the food the other person is eating and desire to eat the same or better food. You only look outwards; you are not able to see that you are much better inside. Envy, jealousy and greed all create different attachments and associations, and you are unable to realize that.

Stepping into the depths of the mind

To understand the subtle behaviour of mahat, you have to adopt the process of introspection, reflection and meditation. Meditation not as it is generally perceived, but the sequence of meditation defined by Sage Patanjali in the *Yoga Sutras*. For him meditation begins with pratyahara and not with dhyana. Meditation is not just closing the eyes, but it has to be understood as a means to discover the beauty within. It is through the sequential practices of pratyahara and dharana that one can go step by step into the depths of the mind and

23

discover where one is connected positively and where nega-
tively. If there is a negative connection, make the attempt to
alter it and if there is a positive connection, enhance it. That
understanding and recognition is acquired only in pratyahara
when you have filtered all the mental processes, observed the
unknown, and can control and guide these processes.

Stop your thoughts for a minute. See if you can do it. For
sixty seconds, be thoughtless. Can you do it? No. Then how
can you say that you are a meditator? If you had perfected
pratyahara, you could stop your thoughts not only for sixty
seconds but maybe for sixty days. Focusing or dharana is another important step. If you have to sit for half an hour with
eyes closed, after ten minutes you are dropping to the left,
right and centre. You go to sleep and later say, "Oh, I had a
wonderful meditation." Sleep becomes meditation for you.
People find it hard to keep their eyes open even in satsang
and they want to remain alert in meditation. Impossible.
They cannot do it. Those who have no control of the mind
cannot practise meditation.

24

If someone who had perfected pratyahara and dharana was asked to meditate for six hours, you can be sure that they would not doze for even a single second and the length and span of their attention and awareness would be constant from beginning to end, no spikes, no wave form. If you can do that, then you can be called a meditator and meditation will have a meaning for you. But if you practise meditation merely for closing your eyes and losing yourself, that has no meaning. Most people who meditate have no control over the mind; their mental states sway their mood in what they call meditation.

When you are able to meditate, realizing properly and fully well that the expressions, nature and behaviour of aham-kara, chitta, buddhi and partially manas (as manas is only the playing field of the other three) have to be understood, analyzed, altered and transformed, you make the attempt to go to another state of mind, which is dhyana. That is when meditation becomes relevant, otherwise stick to pratyahara and dharana.

Sage Patanjali realized this. That is why he emphasized the roles of pratyahara and dharana. The meaning of pratyahara is withdrawing the senses from their associations. In the system of mind management, Sage Patanjali has placed pratyahara and dharana before dhyana. If dhyana had been important to him, he would have ignored pratyahara and dharana and instead of eight limbs of yoga there would be six limbs: yama, niyama, asana, pranayama, dhyana and samadhi. He real-ized the validity of disconnecting the mental processes from their associations so that the mind can be freed from negative expressions and behaviours, and the positive qualities of the mind can be cultivated. Therefore, in the management of the mind or head, pratyahara and dharana play a major role.

Destress, witness, harmonize
How can you cultivate the faculties of the head? First of all, destress yourself. If there is stress in you, you cannot cultivate any faculty. Therefore, destressing is necessary. After you

have destressed. Then begin the process of observing your responses and reactions, and balancing and harmonizing them.

Destressing takes place through the first practice of pratyahara, which is yoga nidra. Then follows observation and analysis of responses and reactions. This can be done by observing your day before you go to bed and watching what has happened in your life on that day in the form of a movie. When you go to bed at night, for five minutes let the movie of the day flash through your mind. "I woke up at this time, then I did this, then I did that, I spoke to this person, it was a happy day, it was a bad day." If it was a bad day, ask yourself why it was bad. Were you in a negative mood? Was the other person aggressive? What happened? You have to see everything. After you have acknowledged everything, question yourself: "If I confront the same situation tomorrow, how can I improve my response to it?" Try to discover this, don't say, "I can't think." If you cannot think, it means that you don't have buddhi. God has given buddhi to every individual, but you identify with the problem so much that you forget the solution. If you don't identify with the problem, you will find a solution. That is the nature of life. Life never leaves you hanging anywhere; you hang yourself.

I've never had any problems in my life, because whenever there was a problem, solutions would come. I never had to ask my guru, "I'm experiencing this problem, what is the solution?" I never asked him, "I have pain in my knee, what can I do for it? I'm having this experience, is it good or bad? Today I saw angels and demons in meditation, what should I do?" I never said such things to my guru, because the way he has trained me is: "If you have a problem, discover your own solution." That is what I apply in my life. Therefore, I often say to people who come to me with their problems, "Don't tell me your problems, tell me what the solutions are. If you are sick, you have to treat yourself. I can only advise you. If you are thinking too much, don't think too much. If you are depressive, be happy, do kirtan, jump and dance. If

26

you've had a tiff with somebody due to a clash of egos, go and shake hands." I can only tell you that much, but the basic fine-tuning has to be done by you. If you can do that, you will be out of difficult situations. If you are unable to do it, a small problem will turn into a mountain.

Practise reflection and analysis of the events that took place during the day and ask yourself if you encountered the same situation again, how you could respond in a better way. Ask yourself, "Can I respond in a positive way? Can I respond in a constructive way?" Think about it. There are four ways of finding a solution to a problem: sama, dama, danda, bheda. Don't ask me what they are. Find out for yourself!

Probiotic yoga

Understand and recognize your responses to different situations. Destress yourself, observe the events and activities of the day. That is the beginning of managing the problems of the head. If you can do these two things, I can assure you that

at least sixty percent of your head problems will be solved. However, you have to do this religiously.

If you get a fever, the doctor prescribes a course of antibiotics. You have to take that course for a certain number of days without any break. You can't stop the medicines in between. The same principle must be applied to yoga practices. Just because you feel lazy today or were not able to wake up in the morning, you say, "I won't do my yoga today." This means that you are not taking your medicine for the day. You are negating your medicine for the day, your antibiotic. Of course, yoga is not antibiotic, it is probiotic. If you can take your antibiotic for x number of days, you must be able to take your probiotic with the same regularity. This is how one starts the journey in the management of head, heart and hands.

Tangible Head,
Invisible Heart

11 October 2010

In order to manage the behaviours and expressions of the different faculties of the mind – ego, intelligence, psyche and rationality – one has to resort to different practices of yoga.

Basic programming of mahat

Mahat is conditioned. A basic programming in the software already exists in mahat. When you buy a computer, it comes with a pre-loaded software, which is known as the operating system. In that operating system you can install different softwares according to your need. In the same manner, mahat, including manas, buddhi, chitta and ahamkara, comes pre-loaded with a basic software.

The basic software in ahamkara, the ego dimension, is the four basic instincts: craving, sleep, insecurity and sexuality. The source of these instincts is the ego, and they reflect the need for self-preservation and self-continuity. The concepts of self-preservation and self-continuity relate to the effort made to maintain oneself and ensure that the next generation continues. To continue life is a basic instinct.

The instincts also affect the behaviour of the mind. When one of them becomes predominant, it alters the normal behaviour of the mind. If sexuality becomes predominant, it affects the behaviour of the mind and the senses. If craving becomes predominant, it affects the behaviour of the mind and the senses. If sleep or disconnection becomes predomi-

29

nant, it affects the whole process of life, mind and behaviour. If there are insecurities, the whole life pattern and process is affected. Any change in these conditions also creates stress in the mind.

Similarly, the limiting aspect or pre-loaded software of buddhi is attachment. Buddhi, intelligence, is the agency which guides you to attach to the external world of sense objects. It is buddhi which says, "This is nice, accept it, desire it, want it. That is not nice, reject it, eliminate it, ignore it." Buddhi is the medium of interaction with the environment and the world. Attachments are caused by buddhi, not by ahamkara. That is the binding, negative or limiting aspect of buddhi.

Role of Shakti

The four aspects of mahat have both a positive and a negative aspect because they are all forms of shakti; ahamkara or ego is a form of shakti, buddhi is a form of shakti, chitta is a form of shakti, manas is a form of shakti. And Shakti, the primordial power, has two roles to play, to unite and to separate, which is why it is known as Yogamaya.

In the manifest world, the role of Shakti is to separate one from the source. Therefore, a conscious effort has to be made to come back to the source. You have to go against the grain of Shakti, you have to swim against the current of the river. Shakti is taking you in the direction of the material world in the form of Prakriti or maya. Shakti is telling you, "Identify with your environment." It inspires the senses to attach with the world. It inspires the thoughts, emotions and desires to attach with the world, to seek fulfilment in the external world. That is the binding power of Shakti. When She is pushing you into the material dimension, She is binding you to the material plane.

The other aspect of Shakti is the uniting aspect. It unites, pulls you back from the material dimension and centres and stabilizes you in the spiritual dimension. When Shakti pulls you from the material and stabilizes you in the spiritual di-

mension, that is yoga. However, to move from maya to yoga, you have to make a conscious effort. You have to struggle against maya to come to the point of yoga. It is this struggle in the life of a spiritual aspirant which can either make or break the person.

The sequential path

If you want to make yourself, then you have to follow a sequence and a system. If you want to break yourself, then jump in anywhere – practise kriya yoga without any preparation, awaken the kundalini without any preparation and you will land up in a mental hospital. If there is proper preparation, then these practices won't break you, they will make you.

Adhering to a sequence in yoga is most important, which people don't understand. They always want to go on to a higher practice, without preparation of the basics. Those who have followed the basic stages of yoga sequentially have become something in life; they have become enlightened in their own life. Those who have always made the jump in search of a new experience without even realizing their own nature, without realizing the nature of their mind, are even today hopping from one stone to another, and haven't found stable ground. That is the reality. There are ample courses on kriya yoga and kundalini yoga, and everybody comes to them to awaken their kundalini. Awakening of kundalini without managing the head and heart will lead you to lunacy.

Many research studies conducted around the world have stated that the kundalini can take you towards both psychosis and transcendence. In the negative aspect it will lead you to psychosis and in the positive aspect it will lead you to transcendence. You need to be aware of this and then make a conscious effort to move from the material to the spiritual. This is where Sage Patanjali's pratyahara and dharana play an important role in the management of mahat. Meditation is not important. You can ignore mediation, but become firm in pratyahara and then move into the state of dharana.

First practice of internalization: yoga nidra
The first practice of internalization is taught in pratyahara, and that is yoga nidra. Even during this preliminary practice people are not able to control their mental states. How can such people move into the higher levels of meditation? The teacher instructs, "Don't sleep", and no sooner are the words uttered than the student is snoring.

In the early days when I used to give classes, I would find that despite my instructions, people would go to sleep in yoga nidra. I tried many tricks. Once in Colombia, I said, "Today we are going to practise yoga nidra standing up." That was a mistake because about thirty people stood up in a line and

32

the last one went to sleep and fell. It had a domino effect! I realized that people do not have any control over their mental states. If somebody can go to sleep standing up and then fall, I don't think that person can ever practise meditation. Anyhow, yoga nidra is the first practice of pratyahara in which destressing takes place.

Entering into deeper mind: antar mouna

After destressing in yoga nidra, to go into the deeper mind, different practices have to be adopted. One of the most important among them is antar mouna.

The expressions and behaviours of ahamkara, chitta and buddhi first manifest in manas, the playground for the three. In antar mouna, when you begin to observe the inner states and see something, a thought or an experience, you hold on to it and go to its source. You use the thought as a string to go in. Sometimes you go to buddhi because the thought has come from buddhi. Sometimes you go to chitta because the experience has come from chitta. Sometimes you go to ahamkara because the instinct has influenced the behaviour of manas. Through antar mouna you can access buddhi, chitta or manas according to the thought in the mind. This is what makes antar mouna a very important practice.

People think that antar mouna is only a practice of inner silence where one has to observe the thoughts, but that is only its first stage. It is because you have not progressed beyond the first stage that you have not been told about the second stage. Very few take that next step because everybody thinks of the practice in terms of 'observe the thoughts, accept them and then let them go; keep your mind blank'. Nobody progresses beyond this stage. It is a practice which can be the most direct method of accessing buddhi, chitta or ahamkara, if done properly. Therefore, one aspect of the mind is dealt with through antar mouna. We are discussing only a few practices which are the simplest and known to everybody, but you have to understand their importance.

33

Observing attachments: SWAN

When you come to the conclusion that buddhi is attaching you to an object or person, that an attachment is being created, then buddhi as intellect plays another role. It begins to analyze: this is good for me, this is not good for me, this is acceptable, this is not acceptable. You ascribe an identity, a form and a shape to your attachments. When attachment becomes strong, there is identification with the object of attachment as if you own it – the feeling of  'It is mine'. When this idea comes in, it is difficult to become the observer, *drashta*, of the experience.

The first rule of yoga is: cultivate your awareness to such a degree that you can become the observer of everything that occurs around you or within you. The *Yoga Sutras* state (1:3): *Tada drashtu swaroope avasthanam*. The seer, the observer, the individual has to establish himself or herself in the state of mind where nothing escapes the internal vision. Everything is observed. Nothing occurs in a subtle way or any other way. Every event, thought and moment is observed. This happens in a very natural and spontaneous way. You don't have to create tension, repeating to yourself, "I have to be aware." When it happens spontaneously, with ease, you can be the observer all the time. When you struggle with yourself, the observer state is experienced only for a few moments while you are struggling.

There must not be struggle in yoga, only cultivation of awareness. With cultivation of awareness, you analyze your attachments while they are being created. "Is it my infatuation? Is it my need? Why am I associating with this person? Why do I desire this object? Is it my need or my infatuation?" Eighty percent of the time you will discover that it is not your need, just an infatuation, a selfish, self-oriented desire to possess something.

Analyze buddhi by using the SWAN principle: Strength, Weakness, Ambition, Need. What are the strengths of your mind and what are its weaknesses? What are its aspirations? What are your actual needs in life? If you are able to classify your expectations and desires in these four categories, understand yourself in the light of your strengths and weaknesses, ambitions and needs, you can be free from the bondage of attachment. People say, "I have to be detached." How can you be detached? There is no need to be detached from anything, just try to analyze and realize the value of things in relation to your need and ambition. If your attachment is based on your need, it is valid. If your attachment is due to your ambition, you will have to rethink it, because it will not bring you satisfaction. It will not provide you fulfilment. Rather, ambitions and infatuations will only give rise to more ambitions and infatuations. In this way, using the SWAN principle, you can cultivate awareness and manage the behaviour of buddhi.

Accessing chitta: ajapa japa

Chitta is the storehouse of impressions, samskaras and karmas. Chitta is one aspect of the mind which you do not have easy access to. It is very difficult to know or realize what your samskaras are. It is difficult to know what the karmas that you are living are. It is difficult to know what your future expectations are according to the samskaras and vasanas that exist in chitta. Chitta can be accessed by using another practice of pratyahara and dharana: ajapa japa.

Ajapa japa is the practice of mantra with breath awareness. Sit down quietly, and observe the breath moving from the navel to the eyebrow centre. When you inhale, feel the breath come up from the navel to the eyebrow centre; when you exhale, observe the breath going down from the eyebrow centre to the navel. Then add a mantra to the movement of the breath: *So-Ham.* It is the mantra of the breath.

35

As you continue with the practice, you will gradually feel drowsy, as nervous tensions go away with breath regulation. When nervous tensions go away, cerebral tensions also reduce. When cerebral tensions reduce, the mind becomes introverted. When the mind becomes introverted, the connection with the senses is cut off. When the connections are cut off, you feel drowsy. At that moment, you still have one tool with you to remain alert and awake. That is awareness of the mantra. When you keep on repeating the mantra with the breath, *So-Ham, So-Ham, So-Ham*, for fifteen minutes or twenty minutes, the mind moves into a state which is similar to, let us say, a catatonic state. It is a state where nothing moves, you become still. In that stillness, impressions and memories of the past come to the surface. I will give you an example of a true incident to indicate how ajapa works.

Many years ago, an asthmatic person came to the ashram. He had tried every kind of therapy to find relief from his asthma. Bronchial dilators did not work, inhalers did not work, no other medicine worked, and the intensity of his asthma was strong. Sri Swamiji was in the ashram at that time. He said to the young man, "Practise ajapa meditation and stop taking all medication. If these medicines have not worked on you until now, they are not going to work for the next few weeks. Stop the medication and practise ajapa meditation." This man started the practice as instructed, as he had trust and belief in the words of the guru. He stopped the medication and started the meditation.

After about a month or so, he had a vision in his meditation related to his childhood. It was something that he had forgotten about completely, and during meditation that distant memory came to the surface. From that moment onwards he was free of asthma. Since that day, that person has not had a single attack of asthma, and this incident took place about twenty-five years ago. When the person went back to his country, he underwent a test to check whether he was actually cured of asthma or not, the Ventolin Challenge Test. It indicated that he was in the clear.

Where medication did not work, meditation did work. It worked because the process was able to bring up a memory which had been the cause of the problem. After acknowledging that memory, acknowledging the suffering and pain in that memory, the person was freed.

Ajapa japa is a good practice to draw out the memories, impressions and samskaras which are affecting your external behaviour. Ajapa japa also centres you in your own spirit, heart and mind. It is a practice which has been eulogized in the vedic and upanishadic literatures. It has been given the most prominent place in the spiritual scriptures because of its ability to clear the inherent and latent impressions, samskaras and karmas.

Understanding symbols of consciousness: chidakasha dharana

A practice of dharana is also used to deal with the deeper mind. As you access the deeper mind in ajapa japa, the information comes to the surface in the form of symbols. Therefore, you need to be geared to understand the meaning of those symbols.

Words are only used to convey something to another person, but how do you think internally? Do you think in the form of words? No. You think in the form of words only when the impression comes to the level of manas. Before that, the form of thoughts is not words, but symbols. The psyche is guided by symbols because that is the language of consciousness. Words are the language of the senses and symbols are the language of consciousness. However, you tend to relate the symbols to things that you already know.

If you see a symbol or image in meditation, buddhi or the intellect immediately kicks in and says, "This is a nice image. I like this image. I feel peaceful when I see this image." As buddhi has come into play, the effect of the symbol is no longer there. It has only become a form which you like. You see another image and buddhi says, "No, I don't like this image. It is ugly, bad, dark, negative." Buddhi stops your understanding and observation of the symbol that has come up and therefore you are not able to eliminate the latent impressions.

The method to understand the language of symbols and bring them to the surface is chidakasha dharana. In the first stage of the practice, you create your own images in the mind, you write your own pictures in the mind. This allows you to develop an ability to understand the meaning of symbols when they come from the depths of consciousness. In the practice of chidakasha dharana, the teacher will at first say, "Draw a symbol in your mind: a triangle, another one, another one, another one. A square, another one, another one, another one. A circle, a star, the numbers one, two, three, four." In this way, the practitioner is taken through

38

a sequence of creating symbols in the mind. When you are able to develop your awareness to the extent where you can remember everything that you have created, you stop creating the symbols and just allow the internal ones to come up. When they do, at one level of the mind you begin to understand what they mean to you, provided you are able to keep your intellect out of that awareness.

Completing the statue

Ajapa japa and chidakasha dharana are practices of pratyahara and dharana to go into and realize the psyche. The SWAN principle is the way to manage buddhi; yoga nidra and antar mouna are methods to access the ego.

These practices, provided you do them consistently, will confer many benefits. But remember, all this takes time. Start your journey before your head becomes too crowded and clouded by the inputs of the world. Always remember that construction takes a lot of time while destruction doesn't take any.

If you want to destroy a building, it can be levelled completely in one week, but if you want to construct a building it will take months. The same principle applies in life. If you want to create something positive within, give yourself time. Don't expect instant results. If you expect instant results, then yoga is not for you, spiritual life is not for you, go and live happily in society. You have to invest time in construction. Nothing comes readymade. Spend ninety percent of your time in construction – creating, developing and nurturing the positive and uplifting, and you can spend ten percent of your time in destruction – destroying what is detrimental, limiting, hopeless and unnecessary. That is how yogis live, while bhogis spend ninety percent of their time in destruction and ten percent in creation.

That is not accepted in yoga, for yoga is a discipline. It is not a practice for enjoyment. It is a serious discipline and you have to understand and accept it as a serious discipline. Don't be whimsical about your practice – "Today I am going to do this because I feel like stretching." All that is fine, but at the same time, be sincere about your practice and commitment. Make the extra effort to construct a better you. Don't think that a better you can be obtained easily. Even a sculptor first finds a misshapen piece of rock, then works hard at chiselling and hammering it until the desired image manifests. If the sculptor does not use the chisel and hammer, the desired image will never be seen. The rock will always be a rock, maybe with a few dents here and there where the sculptor tried to use the chisel. Quite a few people arrive with chisel marks on their faces, but they have not actually completed the full image. Therefore, try to complete the full image. Try to be the full image, and you have only one lifetime to do it.

The invisible heart

There are two hearts: one on the left side, which is the physical heart, and the other on the right side, which is the spiritual heart. The left heart beats boom-boom and is responsible for circulation, while the right heart beats sound-

lessly and is responsible for? Think about it! The right heart beats and another circulation takes place, not of blood, but of *bhava*, sentiment. It is this sentiment, this bhava, which connects you with everything, the visible and the invisible, the seen and the unseen. The expressions of the left heart are material and physical in nature; the expressions of the right heart are transcendental and spiritual in nature.

When you see your beloved, the left heart begins to pound and when you see your God, the right heart begins to pound. When you see your beloved, the left heart says, "I love that person." When you see your God, the right heart says, "I am one with that person." The left heart always maintains duality: me and that, me and him, me and her. The right heart is always united: "I am one." That is the sentiment. Of course, this is not a physical experience. These examples are being used to define the different qualities of the heart. One is a physical organ and the other is the actual energy of the heart.

Bhava, sentiment, is the most important aspect of the invisible heart. The invisible heart beats to the sentiment which manifests when you encounter something pleasant, beautiful, unique, divine and transcendental. What are these sentiments, these bhavas? A sentiment represents a mood of the mind. If love is a sentiment, it influences the mental behaviour. Compassion as a sentiment alters the mental behaviour. Affection as a sentiment alters the mental behaviour. Even anger and aggression are sentiments that alter the mental behaviour.

Open-heart surgery

In the Indian tradition, nine major sentiments have been defined. They reflect the nine moods of the mind. These moods are not guided by buddhi, chitta or ahamkara, but by the sentiment being generated in the heart. How do you recognize that these sentiments are appropriate? The way to measure the quality of a sentiment is that it must have beauty and love in it. A sentiment without beauty and love is

41

destructive. A sentiment filled with beauty and love is constructive. That is the only measure of a positive sentiment and a negative sentiment. When a positive sentiment arises, then the heart opens up and what Sri Swamiji describes as 'open-heart surgery' becomes possible. With the opening of the heart, all limitations dissolve and you are able to connect with every being.

There is one example from Sri Swamiji's life which I feel is most appropriate in illustrating how love can extend beyond physical boundaries. When Sri Swamiji was doing his panchagni sadhana in Rikhia, for nine years he was totally isolated from everything. Nobody was allowed to see him. He was in complete seclusion and did not have any means of knowing what was happening in the world: no radio, no newspaper, no television. One day, after he had completed his sadhana, he came out, called Swami Satsangi and said, "In a nearby village, an accident has taken place. There was a fire in the village." Now listen carefully to what he said. "There was a fire in the village. Houses have burnt down. There is one family in that village whose house has been totally destroyed and the husband has died in the fire. The wife has become a widow. She has three small children. She is sitting under a tree with them. Locate her and help her." This was said by Sri Swamiji when he came out of his sadhana.

How did he know in his sadhana that a fire had raged through the village? How did he know that somebody had become a widow, had three children who were crying because their father had died, had lost everything and needed help? It took us one week to find that village and locate the family. After locating them, we constructed a house and provided all that was required for them to restart their life. For days thereafter, I continued to wonder how Sri Swamiji came to know of this tragedy. Then, one day, somebody asked him a question during a satsang, "Does God hear our prayers?" Sri Swamiji said, "Yes, God hears all prayers. God hears all prayers and if He answers your prayer, it is not because He is happy with you, but because He wants to enforce your faith in Him. If you pray for something and it is fulfilled due to the grace of God, it is only because God wants you to develop and intensify your faith. If you pray to God and He takes time to help you, it is because He wants you to cultivate patience. If you pray to God and He doesn't answer your prayers, it is because He knows you are capable of doing things yourself and do not need His help. If you pray to God and there is nobody nearby to help you, God will inspire someone who will come to you and help you out."

After listening to this answer, I understood what had happened during the incident with the lady. She had prayed, "God, I have lost everything. My husband is dead. I have nothing, only the clothes on my body and these three little children, and there is nobody to help us out. Please help." God heard this prayer. He looked down. Who is nearby who can help this person out? He saw Swami Satyananda and said, "Swami Satyananda, I am forwarding this prayer to you. You organize the needful." When God forwarded the prayer to him, Sri Swamiji was able to see the whole episode in meditation and came out and said, "Go and help this person", giving the details of what had happened.

The real love of the heart is realized only when there is a connection with God. Otherwise, what you experience is sensual and sensorial love, nothing beyond. Your concept of love is not a connection with the divine through which you can spread love all around.

Energy in motion

When the bhavas are material in nature, it becomes difficult to manage emotions. The word emotion is used so frequently, but do you know what the meaning of emotion is? Energy in motion, e-motion. When this raw energy becomes active, you cannot control it. One cannot control aggression when it flares up. One cannot control fear when it flares up. One cannot control insecurities when they flare up. They are all emotions, energies in motion, and they are all raw energies.

43

These raw energies can take you to the material dimension or to the spiritual dimension, because energy has two forms: yoga and maya. Emotion can bind you to the outer world, or it can detach you from the outer and connect you with the inner world.

Emotions need to be balanced and harmonized. In the yogic tradition, nine steps have been taught to manage emotions. These are the nine steps of bhakti yoga, just as there are eight steps of ashtanga yoga. Ashtanga yoga consists of yama, niyama, asana, pranayama, pratyahara, dharana, dhyana and samadhi. In the same manner, in bhakti yoga there are nine practices or stages that one has to go through in order to purify the sentiments, harness the power of emotions and rechannel them.

Focused Heart,
Creative Hands

12 October 2010

The concept of heart in yoga refers to two hearts, one which is physical and the other which is subtle. The physical heart is responsible for the maintenance of the physical body and the subtle heart is responsible for the management of life. Yoga looks at the expressions of the heart from this perspective.

Colours of emotion

When the term heart is used in yoga, the reference is not to the physical organ, but the subtle one which contains the emotions, both positive and negative. Here, the emotions are in their raw form. What goes to the level of mahat – aham-kara, buddhi, chitta and manas – is modified emotion. The emotion has already been trimmed and designed to fit in the specific area of the mind where thoughts, feelings and desires manifest. When generated at the heart level, prior to reflecting in the mind and changing its mood, the emotion is pure, raw energy. The strength of that energy is such that it can carry you with it and make you forget everything else except what that energy is focused on. Anger, infatuation, envy and jealousy are all expressions of this raw energy. Of course, the mind and the heart are not separate functions in terms of emotion, but yoga perceives them as separate entities. The heart has a greater role to play in the life of an individual, in redirecting and rechannelling the outward flowing emotions towards the inner self.

45

When it connects with the external environment, the heart evokes certain responses, based on the contact or association with a sense object. Sri Swamiji says that emotions are totally pure. They are pure energies, untainted by material or personal aspirations and ambitions. In their raw form they are like a crystal ball, totally colourless, transparent and clear, but what happens when you place a crystal ball on an object? If you place it on a red cloth, the colour red is reflected in it. If you place it on a black cloth, the colour black is reflected in it. If you place it on a blue cloth, the colour blue is reflected. The crystal ball in itself has no colour, but absorbs the colour of whatever object it is placed upon. The same applies to human emotions. They are colourless, but take on a colour when associating with an event, idea or object. That colour influences the mental behaviour.

Imagine that you are walking along a road. Suddenly you spot a bag full of money. You will not be able to ignore it. When you look at this bag of money unclaimed by every passerby, which emotion becomes active in you? Greed. As long as you did not see the bag, greed did not exist. The instant you see it, a response is generated in the mind and the heart. The mind says, "Take it, nobody's claiming it", and the energy of the heart takes the form of greed. When you see a small infant, what emotion is experienced? Affection manifests naturally. You don't have to force it; it is a natural response to feel affection upon seeing a child. Similarly, when you see somebody you dislike, the natural response is animosity and rejection. When you see your beloved, the natural response is passion and the desire to be together.

In this way, as the mind associates with different sense objects in the environment, specific emotional responses are felt by the individual. The emotions take on different colours, but in their natural state they are colourless.

Guiding emotions

The way to awaken the positive qualities of the heart is to divert the extroverted emotions towards the self. When

emotions are extroverted, there is always a negative or self-centred response from the emotion. When the emotions are guided towards the self, the response is balanced and harmonious, and guided by inner wisdom. In this case, the negative responses do not affect the behaviour of the emotions.

When emotions are harmonized and pacified, the mind is automatically directed to imbibe virtuous qualities. It is directed to imbibe the good, the positive, the constructive and the creative. Uplifting emotions then play an important role in life. The way to manage emotions, to understand them and guide them has been defined in bhakti yoga.

Bhakti marga and bhakti yoga

Bhakti is seen in two forms. One is *bhakti marga*, path of bhakti, and the other is *bhakti yoga*, yoga of bhakti. Bhakti marga is the ritualistic path adopted by different religions in the form of prayer, worship, adoration, repetition of mantra, and so on. The Indian system of thought makes a distinction between bhakti marga and bhakti yoga and the scriptures indicate this clearly. In the *Srimad Bhagavatam*, bhakti marga has been described when the ninefold path of shravanam, kirtanam, smaranam, padasevanam, archanam, vandanam, dasyam, sakhyam and atma nivedanam is explained. The first six stages here are different external rituals that one has to perform to connect with the source of divinity. They allow one to develop a relationship with the object of one's worship, experienced in the seventh and eight stages. Finally, complete surrender comes about in the ninth stage.

Bhakti yoga, on the other hand, is a path in which you observe and redirect your emotions by changing the conditions where different emotions are evoked. Those conditions have to be changed and the fluctuation between emotions has to cease. The yogis said that in order to perfect bhakti, you have to fine-tune your life, your environment, your mental

and emotional behaviours. Thus, bhakti yoga is a process of personal observation and modification of the destructive and detrimental states, conditions and behaviours, and understanding what is right and what is wrong for you.

The religious aspect of bhakti begins with *shravan* and *kirtan*, listening to and chanting the Lord's name. The yoga aspect of bhakti begins with *sanga*, association. Remember, bhakti in itself means purification of emotions, but when religions took components of bhakti into their fold, they had to turn it into an external ritual which could connect one with the object of one's adoration. That is why there is the rosary, prayers, mantras eulogizing deities, and many external rituals that are performed with the idea 'I am connecting with God'. That connection with God is a religious connection. One identifies with modes and places of worship and makes them the medium to offer one's respect. That is religious bhakti, not yogic bhakti.

Sri Rama's teachings of bhakti

Yogic bhakti is a process of transforming the personality. The concept of yogic bhakti has been defined by Sri Rama in *Ramacharitamanas*. He speaks of bhakti to transcend the self. In this description, Sri Rama says the first method to imbibe and perfect bhakti is observing one's associations.

If you associate with good and pious people, you will also become good and pious in due course. If you associate with negative people, you will imbibe their mentality, thoughts and feelings, and also become negative and destructive. Therefore, seek the company of the pious in life – people who can inspire you, encourage you, who are virtuous and don't commit any wrongs. That is the first condition that Rama describes to Shabari for perfecting bhakti: *Prathama bhagati santana kara sanga* – associate with the pious to become pious in heart, thought and deed.

The second point that Sri Rama makes is: *Dooji rati mama katha prasangaa* – "The second step is love for my stories." People while away their time in unnecessary and idle gossip, discussion and debate, only to prove their supremacy, "I am right and you are wrong." Criticism, gossip and unnecessary chatter are worthless because they do not provide any inspiration. They do not provide any indication of methods to sublimate your energies. Therefore, spend your time thinking, reading, discussing, analyzing and experiencing the existence of the divine spirit. Instead of novels, read scriptures. Novels are mere mental entertainment, but if you read

49

a worthwhile book, you will derive inspiration and education which will help you progress in life.

When you read about the nature and quality of God, the Self, the universe and the world, then you can cultivate an awareness of where to stand in life. Life has been given to you as a process of evolution, and you have to help that process take place. Life has not been given to be wasted in petty gossip, jealousies, hatred and anger. There is a definite purpose to life which has to be lived and realized. Therefore, reflect on and study the literature that can give an insight into your own nature, the nature of the world and the higher self. This is the second aspect of bhakti in yoga.

Sri Rama's third step in bhakti or emotional management is, become humble, egoless. Becoming completely egoless is not possible, but you can at least become free from your arrogance and inner rigidity. Arrogance means that you are rigid inside, there is no flexibility in you. Become flexible internally and reduce the intensity of the arrogance, *dambha* and *abhimana*. Become humble.

Sri Swamiji used to teach me many things in a very natural and spontaneous way. He would tell me, "Even if you think you know, and even if you are capable of doing something perfectly and properly, always think that you do not know, so that every action of yours holds your full awareness." If you think you know, then your awareness is separate from the action. When awareness separates from action and action stands alone, arrogance surfaces in the form of, "I can do it." You identify with the expressions, "Who are you to tell me anything? I know better than you." That is the beginning of arrogance. Sri Swamiji used to tell me, "Even though you may be an expert in anything and everything, always think in your mind that you are only a novice." I have followed that instruction of my guru. Humility, by adhering to the instructions and guidance of the master or the teacher, should be cultivated. When you become humble, then the negative expressions of the heart disappear and the positive expressions manifest. Envy, greed and jealousy disappear; love, compassion, sympathy and affection replace them.

From this perspective, the yogic concept of bhakti is actually psychological development and upliftment of the individual. It fine-tunes your nature to improve the quality of the heart expressions. The faculties of the heart are cultivated by following the yogic path of bhakti, as defined by Sri Rama. Once you have established yourself in this path, then emotions are channelled and redirected towards the discovery of the inner self. When the inner self is discovered, there is realization that it is a reflection of the transcendental self. That is the culmination of bhakti.

The first step is analyzing your associations: the people, family and friends with whom you interact. Ask yourself what kind of discussions and conversations you have with them, what kind of interactions you have with them. You may discover that those associations are not really helping to uplift you. Rather, they are making you more involved and engrossed in the material dimension. If this is the case, you have to separate or distance yourself from those restrictive and negative associations.

Patanjali's guidelines on association

There is a sutra in the *Yoga Sutras* which also puts down the rules of association (1:33):

Maitrikarunaa muditopekshaanaam sukhaduhkha punyaa-punya vishayaanaam bhaavanaatashchittaprasaadanam.

In relation to happiness, misery, virtue and vice, by cultivating the attitude of friendliness, compassion, gladness and indifference respectively, the mind becomes purified and peaceful.

This statement is also an indication that your associations should be appropriate. Be friendly with those who are happy and their happiness will come to you, you will share in that happiness. Don't be friendly with those who are unhappy because their unhappiness will come to you. Be compassionate to those who are suffering, whether mentally or physically, externally or internally. Be happy for those who are virtuous in life and associate with them. Ignore the negative, crooked and destructive. Don't have anything to do with them.

Objectively analyze yourself and the people with whom you associate, then decide who are those who have a positive influence in your life and who are those who have no relevance in your life. Who are those who inspire you to discover a new and positive perspective? Who are those who entice you to become more involved and engrossed in the material dimension? The thinkers have gone to the extent of saying that your association has to be so appropriate that you have to be ready to shun even your partner if he or she is not assisting in achieving the goal.

In this way, bhakti yoga, not bhakti marga, becomes the method of attaining purity of emotions, beginning with identifying your associations.

Realm of higher love

The purpose of bhakti yoga is to attain purity of emotions. When this is achieved, you are able to connect with the environment and people, and understand their needs as your own and your attainments as their attainments. The mind becomes connected with each and every person, and that is when the true and pure expression of love is realized. That love is not physical, carnal or emotional. It is universal and transcendental.

You may have read stories about how in the ashrams of enlightened rishis and masters, animals forget their differences. The tiger and the goat will drink from the same pool of water at a place where an enlightened being practises austerities and tapasya. The animals forget their own natures because of the impact of the environment. The compassion and love there is so strong that the aggressive and fearful natures are forgotten. You may have also had similar experiences before a master. You suddenly feel at peace. You suddenly feel that all your anxieties and worries have dropped away. You had many questions, but now you have none. The mind feels totally relaxed and you say, "It is a very peaceful environment. I had so many questions in my mind, but now I can't think of any." That is due to the subtle love emanating from the yogi or sadhu, which smooth out all the wrinkles of the mind.

Creativity in action

After purity of heart has been attained, then the behaviour has to be fine-tuned to awaken the faculties of the hands. Hands mean action. They represent creativity; they are symbolic of efficiency, excellence, perfection, karma.

Your actions should be guided by creative principles, they must become creative. Creativity is the beginning of attaining the positive qualities of the hands. This is where the concept of karma yoga comes in. Perform actions, whether physical or mental, psychological or spiritual, do whatever you need to, but do not expect anything from your actions. Don't look at the outcome. Try to do your best and develop immunity to the responses of the behaviour or action.

Elation of non-expectation

When I first came to the ashram as a six-year-old boy, whenever Sri Swamiji would ask me to do something, I would run to finish the job and then go back to him. He would only ask, "Completed the job?" I would say, "Yes, Swamiji." He would never say, "Very good." He would say, "Okay, this is the next job."

Much later, when I was older, I realized that after completing a job, my expectation was to receive a pat on the back. That was my expectation and I never received it. What I am indicating is that even with guru, there is expectation. When you work in society, there is of course expectation for money, recognition, name and fame, which is an even worse condition. But even with guru, when one is asked to do something, one may do it to the best of one's capability, but at the back of the mind the idea is, "I hope Swamiji appreciates what I have done." That was my expectation too. "I hope he likes it. I hope he will pat me on the back and say, 'Niranjan, you did very well.'" But it never happened. When I realized that this was my expectation, I became very alert. I said to myself, "Hey, I'm expecting this. This is the result that I'm seeking from my karma. Not good." The day I stopped thinking about it was the first time that Sri Swamiji patted me on the back.

Even in the life of a disciple, there is expectation. It applies to all of you, yet you give lectures saying, "Don't expect anything." You have expectations, yet you lecture everybody on non-expectation, because that is what is said in the *Bhagavad Gita*, this is what Swami Sivananda says, this is what Swami Satyananda says. Despite saying all that, deep

inside, the need, the desire for results exists. Even swamis don't perfect karma yoga. I did not perfect karma yoga until I realized that I have certain expectations from my guru.

Transcending boredom

The law of improving your karma is that you do not identify with what you do, yet you give it your best shot, your full creativity. In my life as a sannyasin although I have often lived a routine life, I was never bored in any routine, but I see other people getting bored and fed up. "I have to go to the same office every morning, see the same people, face the same problems . . ." all these thoughts come. "The same job, the same table, the same boring work, writing vouchers and receipts day in and day out." You get bored. When boredom sets in, creativity stops. When boredom sets in, mind management stops.

I have never been bored because right from the beginning I was very aware of a sutra that my guru gave me to perfect

yoga and I followed it. He said, "Think of everything that you do as if you are doing it for the first and last time in your life. Think of every day as the first and last day of your life." Even as a child I used to think every day, "This is my first day in this life and whatever I do, I'm going to do with utmost perfection." Many times I had to draft letters or do other such routine work necessary in the ashram, but I developed a pattern of thinking which I carry even today, "Today is the first day of your life. Therefore, live it well, live it happily and with total creativity." That is why even if I had to draft the same letter twenty times, I never got bored. Each draft for me was the first and the last one. I never got bored with any work, whether it was cleaning, classes, administration, working for Sri Swamiji or independently. This attitude also allowed me to put all my efforts towards doing the right thing in the proper and perfect way.

Developing a new perspective on performance

Karma yoga is actually an attitudinal change in how you look at situations, events and performance. When you are able to truly practise karma yoga, there is no dissatisfaction in life. What will dissatisfy you if everything is being done for the first time and you have given your full input to it? There is no question of dissatisfaction in this case.

Dissatisfaction is experienced when you feel that you have not done enough. Why did you not do enough in the first place? Either because you did not understand the work or you were lazy. Therefore, creativity is the trademark of the faculty of hands. To become creative, initially you have to make a conscious effort. Creativity cannot be achieved without conscious effort. However, such effort is required only for a certain period of time until you become conditioned in the new mentality. Once an attitudinal change comes about, you develop a new perspective on your performances in life.

Be thou a yogi

Through meditation, pratyahara and dharana, the faculties of the head are awakened. Through bhakti yoga, the lower qualities of the heart are removed and the emotions are diverted and made free from the external influences which distort their fluidity. Through developing more and more creativity, the faculty of the hands is realized.

Awakening the faculties of head, heart and hands means that you have to develop and discover a better you. The possibility of becoming better is already in you. The possibility of improvement is constant and continuous; it never ends. You think, "I can't improve any more" only when your mind becomes stagnant. If you can remain optimistic, positive and creative, balanced in emotions and thoughts, then a new you emerges from the ashes of the old you. That new you is the yogi you. You become a yogi. You do not become enlightened or a siddha, but a yogi who has been able to transform the qualities of life, transcend the weaknesses of life and become established in strength of character and understanding of the

57

spirit. This is the yogic journey that Swami Sivananda spoke about, and this is the yogic journey that Swami Satyananda has started us on.